Grief *through*

Grace

A young widow's journey through loss,
growth, and the power of hope.

Stephanie Lodor

Grief through Grace
Copyright 2025 by Stephanie Lodor
All rights reserved

Contents

Chapter 5

Chapter 6

Chapter 7

Chapter 8

To Charlotte and Sarah:
I did it! This book is for you, my loves.
You made me strong.

To Mom and Dad:
Your love anchored me.
I am forever grateful.

Chapter 1

This is Me

"I can do all this through Him who gives me strength." Philippians 4:13

<u>Our Story</u>

Keith and I dated for four years, eleven months, and two days before deciding to get married. The number of successful marriages that he knew was few. So, he had told me for just under five years that he was never getting married. I guess I finally wore him down. We told each other there would be no divorce if we did this. We agreed that our marriage was too important to us to allow earthly things to get in the way. We disagreed with the adage of never going to sleep angry. We found that we could say some really mean things when tired, things we regretted in the morning. We found that everything looks and feels better after sleeping. We always said "I love you" before going to bed.

We hadn't talked much about having kids until about a month before our wedding. Both of us always said that we didn't want children. When we talked about it, he didn't want to pass on "bad genes," and he didn't believe he would live a very long life because most men on his father's side hadn't lived past age 55. He came from a broken home and wanted his kids to grow up with a dad. He felt the pain of not having a dad present and didn't want his kids to feel that same pain. As for me, I was told as a teenager that I would likely need medical assistance to get pregnant. So, I wrote off the idea of being a mom. I believed it was easier to reject the desire than to experience the pain of not being able to be a mom. When we did talk about it, we discovered that we both wanted children in our marriage. Keith was still apprehensive, given his family history, but after I said, "If you are supposed to leave me young, then I want to have a part of you left with me," he couldn't argue.

It took us three years to get pregnant with our first child. During that time, most of my friends and some family members were enjoying pregnancy and parenthood. One of my best friends was pregnant twice before I was able to get pregnant. It was a time of being extremely happy for them but crushed for myself. I prayed so hard that I could be a mom, make Keith a dad, and share our love and life with a baby. Several nights, I cried myself to sleep while pleading with God for this blessing. Finally, after what felt like forever, we discovered we were expecting! I was so nervous I thought that if I turned my head wrong, I'd lose the baby. That didn't happen, though.

In 2016, we welcomed our beautiful Charlotte into our family! She was everything we had hoped and prayed for and much more! She was such a good baby. It's incredible to think about how much you can love another person. I didn't think my love for Keith could get any stronger, but seeing him be a daddy and care for this little baby was amazing! Watching her grow and thrive with us guiding her was a blessing!

This is Me

There were bumps in the road as we went through life, but nothing we couldn't figure out. It was often simply trying to see things from the other person's point of view. Eventually, I decided to leave my job to stay home with Charlotte. After a few failed attempts at working from home, I returned to school to pursue a degree in Biblical and Educational Studies. This would allow us to have Charlotte in a private school with my schedule mirroring hers. It sounded like the perfect plan, with expected completion by the time she started school. My program was so challenging, but I loved the material. I could feel that studying was changing me and how I interacted with my family and friends. I felt peace and was thriving in my relationship with the Lord.

Loss

Shortly after Charlotte turned two, we discovered we were expecting our second baby. I had so many mixed emotions about this. While I knew in my heart that every child is a blessing from God, I couldn't see how I could finish my master's degree while caring for a baby and a toddler. Then I felt terrible because I knew so many women desperately wanted to be moms and couldn't, for whatever reason. I beat myself up for not being as excited as I wanted, but Keith had a great way of calming me. He reassured me that everything would be ok. He assured me we would make it work with only his income, two children, and plans to move into a nice house.

While studying one morning, I read the introduction of the Gospel according to Luke. The first sentence reads, "Every birth is a miracle, and every child is a gift from God."[1] I sat there and stared at those words for a long time. Then, after praying and trying to work through them, I gave all my fears and anxiety about the new baby to the Lord. I felt so much peace and happiness about this new life. God must have big plans for this child! What would they do? Cure cancer? Become a well-renowned pastor? Be one of the best thinkers of our time? Maybe they will be a light source of joy to whoever meets them. Whatever this baby was going to do in the future, we were the parents who were given the awesome privilege of raising this child!

Then Keith started having these "episodes." He said it felt like an elephant was sitting on his chest. He struggled to breathe. He would get anxious about it. He tried several homeopathic remedies, to no avail. He finally decided to see a doctor. He went to urgent care because it was the weekend. They referred him to the emergency room. We went to the emergency room, where they did an EKG because of previous heart problems. It came back in the normal range but didn't look right, and his enzymes were a little high. Yet, the doctor said Keith had pneumonia. He was given a course of medicine to help him get through it, and we left. When things didn't get better after the round of medicine, he followed up with his primary doctor, whom he had never seen. The doctor wanted to check out his heart before exploring potential issues with his lungs due to his previous heart condition and EKG. They scheduled him for a stress test. Keith hated doing another stress test. He was dreading it and was scared he would do poorly and they would not let him leave. Instead of running on a treadmill, they gave him a chemical stress test. After what felt like five hours, we finally left the hospital. The doctor said it seemed mostly normal, but it didn't look completely right.

The next day, Keith wasn't feeling well and stayed home from work. I put Charlotte down for a nap, and he wanted to lie down, too, thinking that taking a nap would help him feel better. I just laid her in her crib and walked over to kiss him and ask how he was. He told me that he thought he was having a stroke. My uncle called a minute later, saying that Keith was heavy on his heart, and asked if everything was okay. He knew Keith hadn't been feeling well. I hurried him off the phone.

In a panic, I called my mom. She told me to give him an aspirin and call the ambulance. He chewed it like they tell you to do when you feel like you are having stroke symptoms. We decided to go to the hospital; I pulled up the car and came into the house to get him. He said that he couldn't get downstairs. He stood up and fell back onto the bed. I called the ambulance at that point. While waiting for them to get to the house, we managed to get Keith downstairs. I called a friend to meet me at the hospital to take Charlotte. Keith went in the ambulance, and I followed.

My friend met me outside of the emergency room to take Charlotte, and I hurried inside the emergency room waiting area. It was so overwhelming. They made me wait a long time before seeing him. They said they didn't have him in the system yet and that I had to wait until he was. After (I think) 30 minutes, I was finally allowed to see him. Keith told me right away that he didn't have a stroke, and he didn't have a heart attack. He had seen one doctor and was waiting for blood work and the cardiologist. That day, we found out that he had an episode with his heart. It wasn't a heart attack, but there was something wrong. Additionally, all the doctors and medical professionals agreed that something was happening with his lungs. The cardiologist suggested that he have an angiogram done to be able to give him a clean bill of health, which would allow them to start looking for what was wrong with his lungs. We talked, and although scary, this seemed like the right step since he hadn't followed up with his heart doctor for several years.

Keith was admitted to the hospital, and they ordered more tests. The next day, I brought Charlotte to see Keith.

We stayed with him for a while and then left at lunchtime. I took her for lunch and then to my grandma's, where she would stay during the procedure. When I came back, Keith was chatting with the hospital chaplain. After she left, we were lying in bed together, talking and watching the Cubs game. The doctor came to explain the procedure before they took him down. When he finished talking, I asked him where I should be if anything went wrong. The doctor looked at me and said, "Nothing is going to go wrong. We're not even going to find a blockage. But you'll be in the family waiting area." Keith and I talked a little more, we prayed, and the transport team came to take us downstairs. When we got to the family waiting area, I kissed Keith and told him I loved him. He said he loved me and he'd see me soon. With tears in my eyes, I tell you that was the last time I saw my husband alive.

While in the waiting room, we heard a call over the intercom for help: "Code blue in Cath Lab 11". My mom asked me what room he was in. I didn't even know what a "Cath Lab" was, so I didn't think anything of it and said they didn't tell me. Soon, someone asked if I was Mrs. Lodor and if everyone there was family (all but one man was). Trembling inside, I just said yes. She told me that there were complications and that when they got in to see his arteries, there were two that were extremely blocked. The one that had the stint put in so many years before was 100% blocked, and the artery that they call the "widow maker" was 99% blocked and just holding on by a thread. When they started to clear the buildup, his heart stopped. They were working on him, trying to get his heart started. She added, "If they can just get it beating on its own, they can do open heart surgery, a quadruple bypass." In those few minutes that she was with us, I felt my whole world crumbling around me. It was difficult just to breathe. They worked on him for the longest two hours of my life. Every fifteen minutes or so, someone would update me on what was happening.

I prayed so hard that God would let Keith live, but I kept coming back to "Your will be done." The medical staff finally came in to tell me that, after all their efforts, his heart just wouldn't beat on its own. The doctor said he would perform an open heart, but it was really important to him that he keep Keith's dignity by not cutting him open to try because if his heart couldn't beat on its own, nothing he could do would save him. I agreed. Keith was so afraid they'd have to do open heart surgery; that's why he went so long without getting checked out. I completely and wholeheartedly disagreed with Keith, but I knew the doctor was right. Keith wouldn't want to be cut open unless it would definitely save his life.

Grief

So, at the age of 31, pregnant and with a 2-year-old daughter, I became a widow. They allowed everyone with us to go back and see him one last time; by then, our pastor, my uncle, Keith's brother, my cousin, and my parents were there. I remember hugging his lifeless body and sobbing into him. I told him that I couldn't do this without him. How am I supposed to raise these two babies without the best part of me? I walked out of the room first. I couldn't breathe in there. The hospital chaplain left with me and tried to put her arm around me. I couldn't even allow her to touch me; I was so crushed. My cousin drove me home because the hospital told my family that I shouldn't drive. My uncle went to get something for everyone to eat. My mom went to pick up Charlotte. I couldn't even fathom how I was supposed to tell this baby that her daddy was dead and never coming home. And although it happened so long ago, even writing the words now makes me cry thinking about having told her.

Over the past five years and even now, there have been so many people who have asked me how in the world I made it through. My quick answer has stayed the same for several years: "You don't know how strong you are until you are given no other choice." And that is 100% true. However, the long answer is to ensure that your community will rally around you when you are low (and that you are willing to rally around others when they are low, too). My church family provided massive support for me. There were so many people constantly praying for me and my family. My cousin and pastor dropped everything when I sent a text (after the nurse's first visit to say there were complications) to sit and pray with me.

I texted my close friends to tell them Keith didn't make it out of the surgery. One of my friends put her sleeping kids into the car and drove an hour to see me and hug me. She didn't respond to the text message; she just showed up. I went outside to meet her, and we just held each other and cried together. I told her that she didn't need to come. She said that she had to come; we are family. This single act of love meant and still means so much to me. It's hard to describe how impactful that was. She couldn't stay long because her kids were asleep in the car, but she made a two-hour round trip to hug me and tell me she loved me.

When people ask what they can do to help someone whose loved one has passed, I always tell them to pray (prayers can be felt!) and to be present. It means the world to people that you would take time out of your day to come to see the person who just lost their loved one. It is a very simple act of kindness and love.

I had so many people who showed up in the days and weeks after to be with me and Charlotte. One friend showed up and spent the afternoon sitting on the floor with us. Another friend came to drop off the most beautiful bouquet of flowers. Her gift of flowers gave Charlotte and me many moments of comfort and peace. Every week for two years, we went to pick out flowers for the house. And even now, I can still remember how my friend's first vase of flowers looked and how beautiful they were.

Many of my friends and church friends would randomly stop by and bring food, a hug, cards, items from the garden, or gifts for Charlotte. The associate pastor took Charlotte and me out to lunch. Another cousin and my brother offered to pay off my car loan. I already paid it off, but the fact that they were willing to do that still means so much to me. The number of people who tried to help take care of us was unexpected and incredibly comforting. I felt overwhelming love from each one and their actions. Being there for others when they are going through a loss is very difficult and uncomfortable, but it is priceless and a lifeline to the grieving person.

The Healing Process

If you are reading this book, it probably means you are experiencing a loss. Grief often feels like drowning in emotions and being so overwhelmed by life that you can't see a way out.

When I was a couple of years into my grief journey, I enrolled in a training program. This program taught students how to act as coaches for leaders and others, adhering to the guidelines of the International Coaching Federation (ICF).[2] It was and is one of the most impactful parts of my journey. By learning the art of Coaching, the student is coached. I didn't know how much I needed it until I was there. I am now an Internationally Professional Certified Coach, amongst other certificates that I have acquired. When referring to "clients" in this book, I mean those whom I have coached in my practice.

In this book, I will provide stories and reflections from my own life, tools that have helped me through, and Biblical promises. The tools will be in two categories: Mindset Change and Emotional Intelligence (EQ). The purpose of this book is to offer you a beacon of life and hope, to guide you through your grief journey, and to encourage you to lean on God during these difficult times. I pray that you will find comfort and strength in these pages and that you will work on your mindset and EQ growth in the days and weeks ahead.

Mindset Change

Understanding our inner thoughts and mindset is one of the ways that we can grow and work through our emotional thoughts. Our self-talk often does not help us grow and may hold us back. Dr. Carol Dweck talks about the two kinds of mindsets that can categorize our internal thoughts.[3] She says that The Fixed Mindset "is believing that your qualities are set in stone," and The Growth Mindset "is based on the belief that your basic qualities are things you can cultivate through your efforts, your strategies, and help from others." Getting locked into thinking that you cannot change or see a way out will prolong your healing process and often lead to feeling stuck. I aim to offer tools you can implement to cultivate a Growth Mindset instead of a Fixed Mindset. By developing a growth mindset, we are allowing ourselves the best possible attitude to face the challenges in life. For example, a fast way to start working on adapting a growth mindset is to notice when you say, "I can't." Replace "I can't" with "I can't yet." We can grow, learn, and change our lives. Please understand that you can do almost anything that you put your mind to; you just must have the right mindset.

EQ Tool

What is EQ? EQ is the abbreviation for Emotional Quotient. Think of IQ, but instead of how smart you are, it is how emotionally aware you are. We are talking about the ability to recognize, understand, manage, and express our own emotions, as well as the ability to perceive and effectively respond to the emotions of others. The importance of EQ is in its impact on various aspects of life, including personal well-being, relationships, work performance, and overall happiness.

During your healing journey, I hope you will implement some EQ tools. I believe the tools will allow you to experience healing in all its wholeness. This is true because it is said that people with a high EQ are more self-aware, able to recognize and understand emotions, and effectively manage their emotions without being overwhelmed. This self-awareness gives you a clearer understanding of your values, strengths, and weaknesses, enabling you to make better choices and decisions that align with your goals and values. Additionally, EQ helps us develop resilience, which is the ability to bounce back from setbacks and adapt to challenging situations, leading to greater psychological well-being.

I have found EQ to be especially important in my healing in several categories. I think that it has allowed me to be the mom that I want to be. Now, I can ask for a few minutes before reacting to a challenging situation and take a moment to make my response purposeful instead of reactionary. I have worked on being responsive instead of reactive, which I was a lot of during the beginning season of widowhood.

When I'm upset about other things happening in my life, I can assess them and tell my girls I'm not upset at them and that I'm working through some other things. I'm also able to feel more comfortable and confident in showing my emotions to them about missing Keith. We talk about him a lot and cry together a lot. For me, it's important to show my girls that it's ok to be sad and show their emotions to loved ones. I have also found EQ beneficial when returning to the work scene. It is challenging to learn a new skill set, try to meet everyone's needs, and allow myself the grace to advocate for myself when needed.

One of the best ways to start working on your EQ is to look at the emotions wheel[4] (see picture below). The emotions wheel is sectioned into the big emotions closer to the center and branching out into the secondary and tertiary emotions that comprise the big emotions.

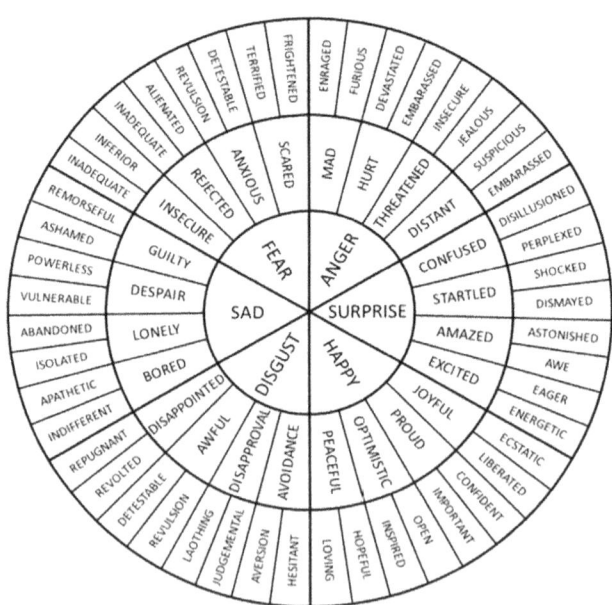

An example of how to use the emotions wheel is to first assess the big emotion you're feeling. With grief, we often feel sad. During those times, I look at the next ring to ask, "What is making me sad?" I know that I have most often felt lonely. Once you're there, you can assess what makes you feel lonely. Initially, I felt abandoned. Later, however, it changed to feeling isolated. And so, you can try to discover why you feel this way. For me, I often felt isolated because, despite having many people around me, there were very few in my immediate circle who knew grief and loss like this. Many of my friends have felt uncomfortable with the emotional onset or remembering Keith. And I know they don't mean to; most people want to be able to fix things, and there is no fix.

Understanding where our emotions come from better equips us to process and move through them.

Biblical Promise

"I can do all this through Him who gives me strength." Philippians 4:13.

As a Christian, and more as a widow, I struggle with this verse so much. I do believe in the promise. What I struggle with is when people confuse this verse with 1 Corinthians 10:13, which says, "God is faithful; He will not allow you to be tempted beyond what you can bear." When people go through something beyond their human ability to handle, they often translate it as "God won't give you more than what you can handle." I cannot tell you how many times I have heard this statement and how many times I have looked back at the person and told them to show me where it says that in the Bible. It doesn't say it. But they mix the two, leaving us with a platitude. This incorrect interpretation insinuates that you are not a good Christian if you're struggling with something unimaginable.

Grief through Grace

The Bible says that if we lean on and into God, He will strengthen us to get us through. This does not mean it will be an overnight miracle in which we suddenly become stronger. No, strength is not grown overnight. It takes many repetitions with weights to get our muscles to grow and change. This is also true for spiritual and mental growth. We use repetition of positive words and beliefs to change our emotions and thoughts. We can say, "God just needs to get me through this minute or this hour." Soon, the minutes and hours will turn into days, and after some time, it becomes easier, taking up less of our mental space and more like breathing. But we can't do it alone; we need to lean on God. John 10:10 says, "The thief comes only to steal and kill and destroy; I have come that they may have life and have it to the full."

I am also not saying that non-Christians can't heal or live after loss or death. Instead, I believe that by trusting Jesus, He will strengthen us. His goal is to give us a full life. I have lost my husband, my soulmate, and my best friend. The pain from that cuts so deep, but I have these two little girls and a full life with them! I am often saddened by what I've lost, and the enemy tries to capitalize on and exploit those emotions. With God's help, I can pull myself out of the sadness and pain and back into gratitude. It is said, and I agree, that the natural antidote for fear is gratitude. When we can recite all the things we are grateful for, what we have, who we still have, and what we have accomplished, we can drive out the spirit of fear. If you struggle with the loss of your loved one and don't know how to get back up from sitting in the mud (so to speak), lean on God and His promises. Ask the Holy Spirit to breathe on you, to take away the fear, and to help you see what you are grateful for every day.

This is Me

<u>Thoughts, Prayers, or Takeaways</u>

_____

_____

_____

_____

_____

_____

_____

_____

_____

_____

_____

_____

_____

_____

_____

_____

_____

_____

_____

_____

_____

_____

_____

_____

_____

_____

_____

_____

Chapter 2

Deciding to Rejoin the Living

"For I know the plans I have for you," declares the Lord, "plans to prosper you and not to harm you, plans to give you hope and a future." Jeremiah 29:11

I am a big fan of Downton Abbey! I love everything about it. It is real and honest and shows how life is wonderful yet tragic, beautiful yet hard! To say that I've watched it repeatedly is an understatement. If you've not seen it, I highly recommend it, but warning: spoilers to come.

At the end of season 3[5], the heir to the title of Lord Grantham, Matthew Crawley, dies in a tragic accident. On the same day that Mary welcomes their long-awaited baby, she finds herself a widow. Mary has a very difficult time coming out of the mist and figuring out how to move forward. Her family and the others in her life see that she is "letting herself be defeated." It's not until one night, when the family pushes her very hard about whether she should take up Matthew's work for the house, that she lashes out and goes to bed. Her grandmother comes to see her and says to Mary, "My dear, you have a straightforward choice;

you can either choose life or death." It is a very hard thing to say (and to hear!), but it is so important to get to the mindset that how we live our lives is a choice. And a part of that choice is whether we will come back to the living. Choosing this is definitely not easy to walk out, but it will be worth it!

I feel like there are two major ways that people deal with their grief: they run or stop. You either make yourself so busy running, running, running that you don't have time to think about how much pain you are in, or you lay in bed crippled by what has just been lost. Both are perfectly fine if you figure out eventually how to come out of that mindset. The problem is that so many people get stuck in their way of dealing with it that they can't deal with the problems and work through the pain. You must decide that you want to heal, that this life is worth living, and rejoin the living. Live your life and enjoy it!

I firmly believe that saying that I'm going to enjoy this life does not mean that I am betraying my late spouse. I honestly don't think that Keith would want me to spend the rest of my life unhappy. I may or may not get married again, but that does not mean that I am unhappy. It means I can and have allowed God to fill that spot, which many of us rely on our spouses to fill—that emptiness and longing for love, to be known fully and still have someone wake up each day and still choose you. It's a hard thing to lose. But God has created me to be who I am despite all my flaws. That's absolutely amazing when you think of it! God looked at you before you were born and said, "I still decide to make you; you will not be perfect; you will not do everything right; you will stick your foot in your mouth a lot! But I still want you and choose to make you!"

Let that sink in for a minute. We don't need a person to fulfill us; we need God to fill us! What is He filling us with?

Deciding to Rejoin the Living

His love, hope, and joy! Being joyful means allowing God to heal your heart, right now in your sorrow and pain, so that the happy is more than the sad.

Deciding to rejoin the living also doesn't have to be done alone. About twenty months after Keith passed away, I had finally decided that it seemed as though I was depressed, like "couldn't come back on my own" kind of depressed. I think anyone would say this is completely understandable, but I had to do something and seek help somehow. I was no longer seeing my grief counselor anymore, which I felt ok with, but I wasn't doing anything more than getting my oldest dressed (because she went to school) and feeding everyone. I went to my doctor, and she agreed with me; she said that depression is a chemical imbalance and that sometimes people are able to get their bodies back to normal, but there are other times when we need to focus a lot on self-care. I was advised to take a break from school, and I started a several-month process of getting better. Today, I still mourn my husband; I miss him so much. It still brings me to tears when I dwell on how Charlotte has now lived longer without her daddy than with him and that Sarah will never know him. She is so funny and has such a great sense of humor. It makes me sad that he never even got to hold Sarah or feel her kick while I was pregnant. It makes me sad when I see something funny on TV, and I reach for my phone to text him still because no one would understand the joke like him, and then I'm brought back to reality.

I could keep going; so many things still make me sad, but that said, they are no longer holding me back. I can laugh with my friends or family and not feel bad anymore. I can share stories, and it doesn't sting like it used to. I can look at my daughters and see how blessed I am to have them without being sad that he doesn't know them or that I don't have him. It took me about five months before I came off the medication, and I have been doing a lot better since, despite the pandemic. I wish he were here with me to talk me through politics, the war in Ukraine, or even the things that were happening during the pandemic. However, I have learned how to find the information and figure it out for myself, who to trust on different topics, and how to stay informed without being so over-informed that it hurts my heart.

Saying that you are going to rejoin the living does not mean that you must stop loving or remembering your late spouse. It simply means that you are not allowing the pain and the hurt to control or stop you anymore. It is there. I don't know if it will ever leave, but it no longer controls. I can do more than sit around dwelling on my loss and my hurt. All the stages of my pregnancy and the first year or so with Sarah were so bittersweet. While I loved this baby and was so happy with her, a part of me felt like everything was just another reminder that Keith wasn't with me anymore. Every time I smiled or laughed or felt happy about anything with the girls, I started crying, too. I sat there crying in Charlotte's end-of-the-year program at her preschool because I got to experience that, and Keith never would have the opportunity to. I was terribly sad that he was no longer here to love on them, to cheer them on with me, and to celebrate them with me. I felt like a part of me was missing with him not being there. It was such a hard season to walk and a lot of explaining why I was crying to a little girl who didn't start feeling the pain of missing her daddy until much later. It is a process to work through; the struggle comes with never working through it.

Deciding to Rejoin the Living

Mindset Change

As the chapter title says, rejoining the living is an active choice, a choice that will bring healing and contentment. My goal for the rest of my life is to be as healed as possible and to be content in all things. Will you join me in that goal? Stating this goal does not mean the journey will be painless, but I believe it is worth it. Here are a few questions we can ask ourselves during a difficult situation. The answers we find can help us form a positive perspective and develop healthy thoughts and steps.

- How can I see this situation differently?
- How will I be able to go on without them?
- What do I need to move forward?
- What would I say to my friend?
- What is holding me back?
- What would a life lived fully for your loved one look like?

Many times in my healing journey, I've had to try to look at the situation differently; working through questions like this can help us get to a better place. It's not easy; it won't always be pretty, neither will the answers. For a while, they will probably feel really uncomfortable asking. Just do your best because little steps over time are a BIG WIN!

EQ Tools

The tool I want to tell you about has helped me so much, and I continue using it. In fact, it sits just behind my computer screen on the wall. I use it when I feel like I'm going to react instead of respond. It helps me to slow down and work through my emotions in a healthy way. I want to share the "Gibbs Reflective Cycle"[6] with you. This wheel works through many questions, but the goal is self-regulation and coming down from an emotionally high place.

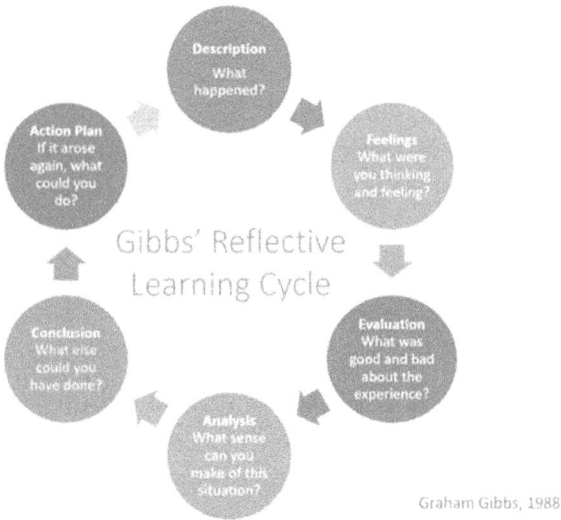

Graham Gibbs, 1988

Often, when we are in an emotionally high or triggered frame of mind, we will only look at the top three questions (making a triangle) and cycle them over and over again. The problem with this is that it doesn't help us get to a resolution of what to do or what we can change. We stay stuck where we are and continue getting angrier about it whenever we think of the situation. If we can slow ourselves down, take a few breaths, and push through the other three questions, we will be better suited to determine how to respond to the situation.

When we can self-regulate, we are able to hold ourselves accountable for the emotions and reactions that we are having and practice being calm. If the situation is really triggering for you and you feel like you can't get through the questions, first decide how emergent this problem is. If you have plenty of time to decide, then read the questions every day and allow yourself to struggle to find your answers. Sit, ponder, and see if you can get any further. If it needs to be done quicker, maybe ask a friend to help you through the questions. Frequently, just being able to say it out loud can really help our perspective and will help us make it through the whole cycle.

Biblical Promise

"For I know the plans I have for you," declares the Lord, "plans to prosper you and not to harm you, plans to give you hope and a future." Jeremiah 29:11

I was reminded of this post from Facebook that I made two weeks after Keith passed. It said,

"It's been two weeks since I had to say goodbye to my best friend, my love, my rock, my soulmate. The only person I chose every day to spend my life with. I got 11 good years of loving him. I was able to kiss him and tell him I love him just before they started the procedure, and I'm very thankful for that. So many loved ones are lost with last words that are not loving. I don't know what God's plan is or why we have to walk this path, but I know he will make good of it. God has given me extreme comfort and peace with this. I'm still grieving and immensely sad, and terribly sad for my little girl who doesn't understand why her daddy isn't coming home, but I have strength and the ability to get up and face the day. I can't always think clearly and sometimes I have to work through things on my own before I can make a reasonable decision on things. Two weeks is not a long time, but this last two weeks without Keith has felt like an eternity. Don't waste a minute with your loved ones. No fight or argument or misunderstanding is big enough to make your heart harbor ill will toward others. God will use this heartbreak for good; Romans 8:28 assures me of that."

So, the first thing I thought when I read this in my memories was that I couldn't believe I was able to be that eloquent so soon after. I remember that everyone was impressed with how strong I was (as if you get a medal for it or something). But I didn't remember typing this and being able to share this message in such a powerful way. I've had so many people who have pushed back on me when I said that I need to get out of my own way and allow God to work through this. It was as if I were saying that God will do all the work and I need to get out of His way. I don't believe that's how it works at all. But I do strongly believe that when God has put a call on our lives that is so far outside of our comfort zone, we often stand in our own way.

"God will use this heartbreak for good." This is absolutely true! But when I felt that God was calling me to write a book... I said back, "I'm sorry. Did you forget who you created? You did not make me to be someone who writes books, stands in front of people, or has the spotlight on myself." That is the last thing that I wanted! I fought it for a year before I gave in and started writing this book! And still, I've been writing for far too long now. But God knows the plans that He has for me!! How incredible is that? And He knew who I was and how long it would take me to get over myself to get to where He needed me to be. How reassuring is that? He's not trying to harm me in this! Jesus said, "The thief comes only to steal and kill and destroy; I have come that they may have life, and have it to the full." John 10:10. God did not cause this to happen to us; Satan comes to steal, kill, and destroy. We need to understand that if we can get out of our own way and out of our own heads, God will make good of whatever happens.

Grief through Grace

Thoughts, Prayers, or Takeaways

_____
_____
_____
_____
_____
_____
_____
_____
_____
_____
_____
_____
_____
_____
_____
_____
_____
_____
_____
_____
_____
_____

Chapter 3

Allowing Yourself the Grace to Face Another Day

*"Three times I pleaded with the Lord to take it away
from me. But He said to me, 'My grace is sufficient
for you, for my power is made perfect in weakness.'
Therefore, I will boast all the more gladly about my
weaknesses, so that Christ's power may rest on me.
That is why, for Christ's sake, I delight in weakness,
in insults, in hardships, in persecutions, in difficulties.
For when I am weak, then I am strong." 2 Cor 12:8-10*

Everyone has a different definition of grace. For this reason, I have a podcast and a blog titled "Discovering Grace." I'm having conversations, discovering how people define grace in their own troubles and trauma. I haven't received the same answer twice yet. For this book, we will defer to Webster's definition. Webster says: "unmerited divine assistance given to humans for their regeneration or sanctification." I usually say that it is an unmerited favor. There is nothing that I did or can do to deserve the favor that I have been given. It is a gift that came at an extremely high cost, yet free to me.

Grief through Grace

When we talk about giving grace to others or ourselves, it takes on a different meaning. I can't, for instance, take on someone else's sins by dying. But what it does mean, at least to me, is to be able to forgive when there's no reason to, to be friendly when everything inside of you is screaming to be as ignorant as others are to you, to trust when trust has been broken, and so on. We often find it easier to give grace to a friend. When someone falls off the map for a while and says, "I'm sorry, life just got in the way," we can be understanding. Or when there has been an argument, we give grace because of the person's difficulties or because we understand what brought this on. We allow the ones we love to use us or have 'bad days' because they know we're not going anywhere, and others won't stick around for that kind of treatment. These are examples of what giving someone grace looks like in our world.

So then, what do I mean by "allowing yourself the grace to face another day"? Most people in the thick of grief and depression find it really difficult to manage all the things that they used to do with no trouble, like keeping house, cooking dinner, personal hygiene, and so on. It's not that you don't want to or that you're not constantly telling yourself that it's not that hard, so just do it. However, motivation or self-push is never enough to complete these daily chores. Giving ourselves grace means not beating ourselves up when chores and other daily activities are left undone.

As I said before, often, we give our friends more grace than we can give ourselves. We hold higher expectations of how we should respond to or handle things than we would expect from anyone else. The first question that comes to my mind about giving ourselves grace is, "If a friend came to me, saying similar things as what's going on in my life, with all the same concerns, what would I tell my friend?" I can't tell you how often I've told my friends to be easy on themselves; it's okay not to make the mark today. Try again tomorrow. That is very true! Just keep trying. Grace, kindness, gentleness, and self-love will carry you until you can fully step back into life. While this is easier to say to a friend, we need to be able to follow our own advice.

Several years ago, one of my colleagues used the term "sitting in the mud" when it came to working through trauma. She said she wasn't sure she was ready to get up and stop sitting in the mud. I think that's incredibly self-aware and hugely profound to me! I've always said "being in the thick of grief" because everything felt muddled and foggy at that point for me. But "sitting in the mud" paints a very physical and vivid picture of what it feels like. And I think admitting that you're not ready to get out of the mud yet is perfectly fine. I encourage you, as you are ready to begin healing, to set a time limit on how long you will allow yourself to sit. It can be for another week or another month, and really, you could say that you don't feel like you're going to be there at any time this year. Okay, that's cool, but make sure we can return and reassess that in the new year.

Nowhere is it promised that this life will be easy, and if you are reading this book, I can only assume you've experienced your fair share of trauma. We are not always going to have good days; we are not always going to have easy days. Some days, we are lucky to make it through the day with everyone being fed before getting back in bed. And that's okay!

One of the top ways I give myself grace is by raising my two strong-willed children, whom God blesses me with. Many times, giving myself grace is simply walking away or asking them to allow me a few minutes to think. In these times, I might feel like screaming or snapping at them. Frankly, kids can be exhausting while grieving. I allow myself to pause so I don't do something that I will regret. I don't want to allow my internal anger to influence my parenting. However, we all know that kids push us in ways we never thought possible and that sometimes we must check ourselves. When I can't check myself because of whatever is happening, I will ask them to go play or suggest they read or draw. This allows me the time I need to deal with my thoughts and emotions before I handle the situation or request. Common examples of building tension are being whined at when I've already given an answer, spilling something, making messes, breaking something, or my own overwhelmed feelings. Sometimes, I'm not in an emotionally regulated space to meet them where they are as children. They are doing everyday childlike things, and sometimes, I'm just unable to meet them there. In those times, I'm grateful to have my parents to help when I can't. I can tell my mom that I just can't or say I'm entirely over the day, and she steps in.

The other day, it was 5:00 p.m., and the day was filled with a lot of crying, whining, and fighting. I asked my mom if it was bedtime yet. I was so over the day. My mom suggested taking the girls to the park. Even on the way, I was still pretty unregulated. However, once we got there, they started playing; I was just able to sit in the fresh air and not have to "go" anymore. I started feeling better, calmer, and more regulated. Giving ourselves grace can mean or look like anything. Taking a few minutes before coming back and dealing with a difficult situation, being able to ask for help, and watching a movie at 5:00 p.m. because I can't do the rest of the day are all examples of what grace looks like in my life.

Mindset Change

I previously stated my first question would be, "What would I say to my friend who is having the same situation that I am experiencing?" Another question that we can ask ourselves to change the way we think about what is going on is, "What do I need in order to give myself permission for this?" Often, the way to give grace is simply to give permission. If the dishes are bothering you but standing to do all the dishes seems impossible, give yourself permission to wash only one or two dishes. Tomorrow, you can try to wash one or two more.

I still work on this a lot, especially during the difficult times of the year, like his birthday, our anniversary, and the anniversary of his death. These are all still very difficult for me. They are not as painful as the first few years, but there are still times that I feel like I don't want to do everyday life. And on those days, I find someplace for us to go, and we get away for a few days. Most of the time, I ask myself, "What is most important for me to get done during the day or week, like the bare minimum? Can I take the week off? Do I have to work on this project or the company? Do we have to work on school?" I typically start looking at these questions about a month ahead, although, with school, it all gets set at the beginning of the school year. I know better now, so I set that we are just taking these three days off.

Changing how we phrase things can give us permission to feel how we feel. This helps me give myself grace and not feel so bad about myself all the time. Being in the mindset of how terrible I am doesn't really serve anyone or do anyone any good. That is not a good recipe for me to be an exemplary mom, daughter, friend, or Christian. Now, don't get me wrong; I often find myself back in this realm of being so hard on myself and feeling like I'm a complete and utter failure. By giving myself grace, I can give myself permission to express my feelings right now and try to count the things that are going right. I celebrate all the small wins (ask any of my friends!), and this is a big reason why. If I can acknowledge and celebrate what is going well, I'm not so focused on what is going poorly. Allow yourself permission for where you are right this minute and try to focus on the good. It can be difficult at first and often can be a challenging skill to develop, but with time and practice, you'll get there!

EQ Tools

EQ tools teach you how to best regulate yourself so you are in a calm frame of mind and can look at a situation in the best light. EQ helps us respond positively instead of negatively reacting to situations. How many times have you flown off the handle and then regretted something you said because you were emotionally heightened? I know I'm not the only one. When we come back down from all the swirling emotions, we can look at the situation differently and think of how to do better. In this section, I will teach you about a good breathing exercise if you have a few minutes to sit quietly to calm down before responding. I certainly know that this is not possible all the time. So, we will look at other breathing exercises in future chapters, but this one is good because it allows for rhythmic breathing and slowness to set back in. It is called boxed breathing.

There's a lot of science behind boxed breathing and its benefits. It is well known for being taught by the Navy SEALs to manage the fight-or-flight response and promote mental clarity. Below are the boxed breathing steps.

- Step 1: Breathe in, counting to four slowly. Feel the air enter your lungs.
- Step 2: Hold your breath for 4 seconds. Try to avoid inhaling or exhaling for 4 seconds.
- Step 3: Slowly exhale through your mouth for 4 seconds.
- Step 4: Repeat steps 1 to 3 until you feel re-centered.

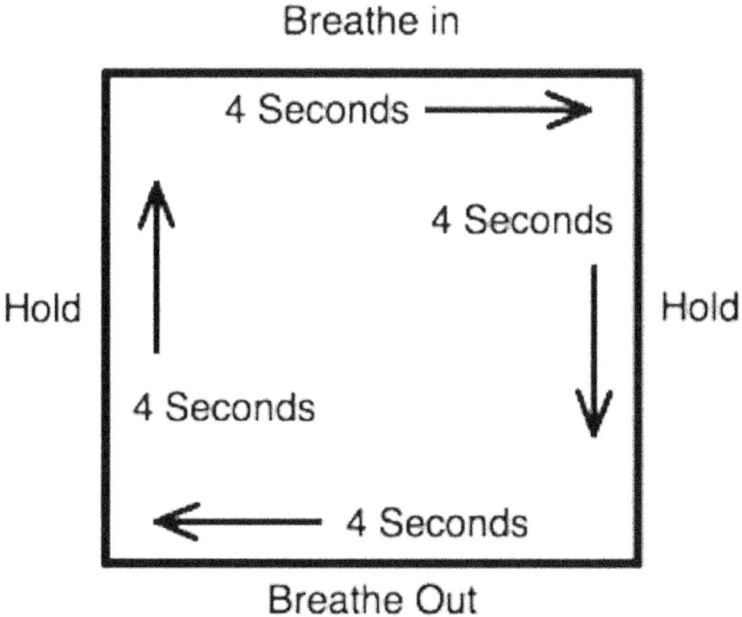

Breathe in

Yes, I actually visualize the box whenever I do this exercise for myself or count someone through it. The visual helps me focus on the box and breathing instead of what is happening, allowing me to calm down. I have seen it help countless clients, and it has helped me and still does. I like to place my feet flat on the ground, sitting straight up so that my back is no longer on the back of my chair, and place my hands palm side up on my legs. We have so many sense receptors, particularly in our hands and fingertips. Positioning our hands this way helps us to avoid distractions and what is happening around us.

Now, I recommend this to everyone, even though I know that there are people out there who hate breathing exercises (my child being one of them), but open your mind to the idea that this can and probably will help. After all, what could it hurt? And we're also trying to work on our mindset, right?

Biblical Promise

*Three times, I pleaded with the Lord to take it away
from me. But He said to me, "My grace is sufficient
for you, for my power is made perfect in weakness."
Therefore, I will boast all the more gladly about my
weaknesses, so that Christ's power may rest on me.
That is why, for Christ's sake, I delight in weakness,
in insults, in hardships, in persecutions, in difficulties.
For when I am weak, then I am strong." 2 Cor 12:8-10*

Paul was telling the church of Corinth about a "thorn in his side." He asked and pleaded with God to take away his pain, and finally, he heard Jesus tell him that God is made perfect through our weakness. We do not encounter these struggles and hardships to break us or even to elevate Jesus. No, we have these difficult times because Satan is a liar, and he desires to steal, kill, and destroy (John 10:10). But if we allow God to work through the hurt and the pain, He is made perfect in our weakness. The enemy will still whisper lies in our ears the closer we get to Jesus, but when we can confront what is being whispered in our ears as lies and deceit, we can walk stronger with the Lord. Jesus told Paul that His grace is sufficient for us. God has so many plans ready for us, but we get impatient or dismiss them as the enemy distracts us. I tell you the truth; if you are walking with the Lord, you can ask for discernment, and He will help you hear His voice instead of Satan's lies.

If your struggles are like mine, I start second-guessing myself and putting myself down. At those moments, if I repeat God's promises, the Word of God realigns my thoughts to view me as God declares me! I can rest again in God's plan for my life. A lifelong lesson of mine is that it doesn't matter what anyone else thinks about me or my plans; as long as I follow Christ, He has it all under control. This truth allows me to release everyone else's strongholds on my mind.

Your struggles could be anything: drugs, money, sex, etc., but there are promises for you. "God's grace is sufficient" (2 Cor 12:9), "I knew you before I formed you your mother's womb" (Jeremiah 1:5), and "I can do all this through Him who gives me strength" (Philippians 4:13). We need to get into the habit of saying God's promises over ourselves and our kids. Can you imagine how much more positive our world could be?

When we take away the demands and expectations that others place upon us, we can give ourselves the grace to be where we are. Now, that's not to say that this is a free pass to just sit in the mud forever, but rather than putting expectations on us, we can view it as an opportunity for growth. Set a time for how long you're going to sit in the mud, then pick yourself up and set goals. Even if your goal is to wash one dish, that's great! Wash two tomorrow. Only wash one load of laundry. Tomorrow, put it away. But often, we see the vast amount piled up because of where we are mentally, and we get discouraged from doing anything. Now, if our friend were in the same situation, most people would give grace for where that person is and how they find themselves to get out of that spot. Yet, we don't allow ourselves the same grace we give others.

Thoughts, Prayers, or Takeaways

Chapter 4

Moving Forward, Not Past

"He heals the broken-hearted and binds up their wounds." Psalm 147:3

There's a great TED Talk by Nora McInerny called "We Don't 'Move On' from Grief. We Move Forward with It."[7] It's amazing! She's funny, and she is so real about grief. She says most of our society thinks we need to just "move on" from our grief or pain, but that's not reality. Grief and memories are carried with us no matter where we go; the experience informs our decisions and everything about us. For example, my marriage to Keith and the life, love, and moments we shared together created who I am today. Nora talks about how emotions are tied around all those memories and how it's okay to feel this way. Not all things can be fixed, and not all wounds will be healed. With humor, she compares grief to having kids. She says that no one sends you a congratulatory card when you have a baby and then, five years later, thinks, "What another birthday party? Geez, get over it already."

So many people in our society think we must move on from whatever has happened to us. "Shouldn't you be over that by now?" The truth is that this experience in your past can't simply stay in your past. We must figure out how to keep moving forward with it, as it will always be a part of who we are. This part of our life will not be erased, and we can't simply stop talking about it. We lived it. Hopefully, we have learned from it and cherish the memories.

People often still show how uncomfortable they are when I bring up memories of Keith. But the truth is, I was with that man for my whole adult life until he passed. He taught me so much and challenged me. He challenged my thinking, which helped me grow into a better person. He didn't just let me be content with the incorrect thinking that I had as a 20-year-old. And he didn't let me sit on my soap box when my thinking was incorrect. He would push my thoughts and try to help me see a better, more correct way. He has shaped who I am now. My ability to love and be loved has been moved and shaped by him, and I will carry him always. How am I supposed to just stop talking or thinking about him? The reason that people are uncomfortable with me talking about him is that they don't know how I will respond, and they don't know what to say to me. They think I will still burst into tears at the mention of his name. But in fact, I enjoy my memories of him and am so thankful for the person he helped me become. That doesn't just disappear when someone dies or leaves our lives; we carry people with us always, even if we don't talk about them anymore.

So, what does it mean to move forward? Moving forward means allowing ourselves to feel what we feel but not get stuck there. This past Easter, in my Facebook memories, I saw a picture that Keith and I took together. It was the last Easter before we became parents. I saw how much love there was between us and how happy we were, and I felt deeply how much I missed him. So, I shared the memory and captioned it with, "Not every day is super difficult anymore, but looking at this picture, I miss my person, and I miss being his wife. *Wife* has been one of my favorite titles." I don't always share my memories or thoughts when I see them, but I always allow for the feelings, whatever they are. I allow them to wash over me, allow myself to really feel them, and then move on with my day. Several hours later, a friend who lives on the other side of the world called me. He said he was stuck in traffic and wanted to check on me. I know he is commonly stuck in traffic and very seldom thinks of calling me because of it. But he called me at that time. Why? Because he saw his friend's post and wanted to make sure that I was ok. What a great friend, right? Now, here's the crazy part: it took me several days to put the pieces together and realize why he called me. Why did it take that long? Because by allowing the emotions, we can move through them so much faster than if we stuff them down and pretend as if they are no longer a bother. By acknowledging them, we allow our mind and body to process what we are going through faster and more easily. We are not triggered and stuck there.

However, we run into several challenges when it comes to moving forward and not backward. The world around you may start to judge that your life doesn't look how they think it should. My dating life is the topic of much conversation, with people asking if or when I'll feel ready to remarry. And the truth is, I'm not opposed to it anymore; I just don't feel that God has said it is my time yet.

Another difficulty with creating a life without my husband is that it has changed my views on making decisions for me and the girls, such as medical decisions, schooling decisions, and whom I allow to be an influence. I'm sure there are many more I'm not thinking of, but those are the biggies. I see the world through a completely different lens than almost anyone else. Everything I do is filtered through the knowledge that the girls only have my family and me; how will this impact us? There are so many things that I took for granted when Keith was here, safety being at the top of the list. I always felt safer when I was with him.

There's so much more that I could babble about on this topic, but at the end of the day, seeing the world through a new lens makes everything take longer and feel more important. But we can keep moving forward even with that new lens. We must understand that it influences our decisions and be aware that it may be incorrectly tainting them. I recently looked at several movies I wasn't allowing my girls to watch. One example of this would be a movie about two children trying to use magic to bring back their deceased father. Such a movie is just not a good idea for my girls to watch at such a young age. They have enough to worry about without having this idea that if they only knew the correct way, they could maybe bring their dad back.

I realized that it was only with this new lens that I feel this way, and I probably wouldn't have felt this at all if it hadn't been for the death of my husband impacting my ability to make this choice. It is not always easy to see how this experience (and the pain that comes with it) impacts us, either good or bad, but I find that I heal a little more once I analyze why I made this choice and whether it is still a good choice. We don't have to try to hide emotions or pretend that this doesn't still affect us, as the term "moving on" implies.

Mindset Change

So, knowing all of this, the challenge is how do we change our mindset and allow ourselves to move forward? As I already said, permitting ourselves to feel what's happening is a good first step. Many of us are afraid to allow big, intense, or deep feelings. We block the feelings or run from them. However, the tool I will introduce will teach us how our brain receives negative words. There is a good short video on TikTok that talks about how the human brain does not understand the negative. The man says, case in point, don't think about an elephant. Of course, you thought of an elephant. The idea is that when we say something negative, our brain crosses out the negative word and is left with the same sentence, just without the negative word. For example, "Don't hit your sister" becomes "Hit your sister." I'm not sure how much scientific evidence is behind this thought, but I can say, as a mom, it seems to hold up. While potty training my younger child, I told her, "Keep your diaper dry" instead of "Don't pee in your diaper." I will talk about how we want to have gentle hands and gentle words. Instead of saying, "Don't treat her that way," I emphasize how she should be treated, or something similar. It works!

We can use the same thought to change our mindset. If we can change the words and phrases we say to ourselves and others, we will train our brains to believe that they are true. The reason that we cannot give ourselves permission for something is that our expectations are different than what has happened. We had on our list to finish the dishes, and that didn't happen. How can we change our expectations to allow for whatever actually happened and be okay with it? We can change the words we say to ourselves. Instead of, "I didn't get this or that done today; I'm such a failure," we can change our words to, "I gave it my all today. I'm ok with what I got done, and I'll try again tomorrow." Working to change the words in our head is not an emotionally easy feat. It can take a long time for our thoughts and our minds to change about who we are. If we keep saying things in the positive instead of the negative, we will eventually change our thought process and start to believe the positive about ourselves.

Working on changing thoughts from negative to positive does not always work for everyone, but I have seen it work with most of my clients. I believe it is worth a shot to see if it will work for you, too. And even if you cannot always go to the positive, it is ok because at least you're giving yourself permission for where you are in the grieving process. As I have said in other chapters, this is not giving permission to sit and never move forward again; this tool is for when you are in the thick of or in the ugly of grief or depression. Everyone should aim to heal emotionally, mentally, physically, and spiritually. But if you're not there yet, it's okay!

EQ Tool

Often, being able to move forward or give ourselves permission is overshadowed by the amount of stuff on our to-do list. At least, that's how it is for me. I get so bogged down with how many things need to get done that I cannot see how to work through any of the things on my list. I become emotionally overwhelmed and stagnant in all the areas of my life. I have started to utilize the tool for this chapter to help me with this. The tool is "The Rule of First Things First." I first heard about this tool on a friend's podcast, *EQ Gangster*, by Noble Gibbens.[8] (It is a fantastic podcast; you should check it out!)

"The Rule of First Things First" tells us that we should list the things we need or want to get done and then work through the list, prioritizing each item. So, if I have a big work assignment due next week, that takes higher priority than continuing education. You focus on one thing at a time by working through and prioritizing the list. This quiets the negative, self-defeating talk and the overwhelming feelings that come with focusing on all the other stuff on the list. You'll get to it, just not yet.

I will say this is probably my biggest area of struggle. Every tool in this chapter is a daily struggle. I remind myself to move forward. I give myself permission to feel in the moment. I replace negative messages with positive ones so I don't always feel like a failure. Lastly, I prioritize what needs to get done in a timely manner. But these tools are not my first response. I stop myself from spinning out of control and grab a tool. I find it challenging to write about the tools when I sometimes forget to put all these things into practice myself, but I'm still growing and healing. I know that all of these tools help. Sometimes, it's just so hard to remember what works and helps when you're in the heat of being overwhelmed, overstimulated, and just plain tired. I'm not perfect, but that's okay! We just need to try again tomorrow!

Biblical Promise

"He heals the broken-hearted and binds up their wounds." Psalm 147:3

I feel like this promise is a bit of a struggle; after all, I begged and pleaded with God to heal Keith. I don't know why the answer was that Keith could not be healed on this Earth, but from other scriptures, I know that Keith is, in fact, healed now. We often struggle when we don't understand why God says "no" to something; we try to figure it out, and we keep holding onto the thing. Over the last ten years, I have come to understand that I won't know everything in this life. I'm okay with waiting until I get to Heaven to ask God my many questions. But this passage assures us that if we allow God to, He will heal our broken hearts and bind up our wounds (whether that's in this life or the next). When this Psalm was written, the Israelites were in exile and working in slavery for the Babylonians. To say that they were brokenhearted is probably a huge understatement. But in their brokenness, we get some of the Bible's most real outcries to God! These people were hurting, and they clung to God and His goodness! In the same way, if we can cling to God and allow Him, He will heal us.

I think this goes back a lot into the mindset that we put ourselves in, but it's so very important! Joyce Meyer calls it "Stinkin' Thinkin'."[9] She says that when we are looking out only for ourselves and how terrible this thing is that has happened to us, essentially, we are being a victim of the circumstance. *Yes, this thing did happen to me, and yes, it will influence everything that is going on in my life and every decision I make for myself and my family.* But the part that people get stuck on is that while this did happen to me, it does not have to consume me! There is so much more to my life than this one thing.

I know that just saying that will not take away the pain. It will still hurt and be so uncomfortable figuring out where to go now and how to navigate life after this loss. However, what it does mean is that when you decide to get out of the mud, you will start to allow God to heal you, and the pain will not consume you anymore. One way Joyce Meyer says we can pick ourselves up and heal from the hardships we've faced is to focus on God and other people. If we are so busy living to tell others about God or serving the purpose that God has put on our hearts, we will become healed and able to move forward with our new lives. God will heal us from this brokenheartedness if we let Him!

Moving Forward, Not Past

Thoughts, Prayers, or Takeaways

_____

_____

_____

_____

_____

_____

_____

_____

_____

_____

_____

_____

_____

_____

_____

_____

_____

_____

_____

_____

_____

_____

Chapter 5

Setting Ourselves Up for Failure

"Trust in the Lord with all your heart and lean not
on your own understanding; in all your ways submit
to Him, and He will make your paths straight."
Proverbs 3:5-6

It seems the older I get, the more and more I am shown my failures. How could I have done better? Society tells us our attention should be fixed on our mistakes instead of focusing on our accomplishments. We live in a state of continuously being beaten down and feeling like we are not enough. Society starts teaching us as kids that we need to look at what is wrong or how we can do better instead of being proud of what we did right. As students, we are conditioned to focus on incorrect answers, thinking, "What did I miss?" That continues all the way through school, and the older we get, the more we play negative self-talk messages. These negative messages hurt us and those around us instead of helping. For example, *my basketball team won the game and then our city championship, but all I could think about were my missed shots.*

As we grow, we become parents, and then it seems that nothing we do is correct. Someone is always coming at you with how it should be done or what they did instead of what you are doing for your children. As women, we criticize and beat each other up. Additionally, social media may cause us to "compete" to make our lives and families look as good as what our "friends" and family look like, even though most of us feel like it's all a big lie and that our family really isn't that pretty, nice, fun, or good all the time.

There are so many examples of how we look at and carry around our failures. A healthier way to live is to trade the standards we learned from society for the standards God provides in His word. Allowing God to fulfill our lives helps us let go of much, if not all, of our failures. As Christians, we believe that we are created in God's image. Without God, we always feel like something is missing from our lives, and we fill that void with all sorts of things: drugs, food, sex, money, and, much to our detriment, our partners. When we allow God to fill us and tell us who we are, we will experience a more meaningful and successful life.

I firmly believe that one of the biggest problems that couples struggle with today is their reliance on their partner to complete them and make them happy. One of the best things that Keith taught me is that he cannot be the source of my happiness. He said, "That's too much to put on someone's shoulders, and I won't be here forever." He encouraged me to learn how to thrive both apart from him and with him, strong by my side.

We set ourselves up for failure when we expect our relationship to be the whole of who we are. What happens when your spouse needs you to give a lot more than they did before? Or you start carrying the relationship because your partner is not in a place to help? Or if your spouse becomes injured, and it affects their mobility? Or something devastating happens to them, impacting their mental and emotional state? And, of course, what if your spouse dies?

What happens if you have a great marriage but are still unhappy? I believe putting all that on your partner is too much. Like this problem, there is another issue that we run into: the fear of being alone. If we let go of finding our self-worth from our partner, we won't be so afraid to be alone. Our worth, joy, and fulfillment should come from God, not another human being.

I do not feel like I must remarry; if I do at some point, that's great! But I am not searching for a new husband or father for my daughters. I told God during the first year after my husband's death that if I decided to remarry, He could bring someone into my life. He brought people together long before the age of online dating; I would not be joining any dating apps. If I'm not supposed to marry again, I'm okay with that because I find my fulfillment through the Lord, not through any human relationships. I have a lot of wonderful relationships without being married. I have amazing friends, my mom and I are very close, and my whole church is a part of my family. All of which ground me in the Lord and help me love, influence, and teach my daughters.

People often struggle with finding their purpose. There are many books out there to help people determine and find their purpose in life. Put simply, one of our purposes as Christians is to tell others about Jesus. One of the most profound teachings I heard from Joyce Meyer was about this topic. I have never heard someone say it so simply. I've always thought the call/job to tell others about Jesus was for people in ministry roles, leaving the rest of us to just go about our lives. As the old hymn says, "They'll know we are Christians by our love."[10] It's a great song, and I think if we show love, even in struggles, it sets us apart. Although, I don't believe it is as simple as just loving. Joyce indicated that we need to share Jesus with people in our everyday lives. If you are a teacher, pray for your students, for an opportunity to share Jesus with them, and love them when others don't.

I know so many teachers. One dear friend walks her classroom praying for the students, praying that they have a successful year, and so on. She is such a light and a beacon to her students! My sister-in-law is a teacher, and one student (not one of her students) called her the "hallway angel" because of her presence and kindness shown by monitoring, helping, and talking with the students in the hallway. If your passion is working with your hands, fixing, or building things, do it in a way that can show Jesus through your work! A man from church works for a tire company, and he often talks about people being blown away by his kindness and not feeling taken advantage of (as so many of us do at places dealing with cars). He said customers often ask him about Jesus, and then he can share with them. If you are a stay-at-home mom, teach your children about Jesus, His sacrifice for us, and how to love others even when it's hard. By finding our purpose with God for our lives and working to fulfill that purpose, we will have joy, peace, and contentment regardless of what is going on in our lives. And that is where true success comes from!

By living our lives in step with our purpose, we will be able to live successfully and struggle less with the feelings of failure.

Mindset Change

Quite often, when we experience trauma, we go down the line of self-doubt, saying, "How is this my fault?" This is a common refrain for people who have gone through major life-altering events. It's our brain's way of processing what has happened to us and seeing if there is a way to make things go back to how they were. Along with this series of thoughts, we are often triggered a lot more (remember that emotionally heightened responses are usually labeled as triggers). We don't understand why we are being irritable or what is going on to cause this trigger. One of the best ways to heal is to understand our triggers and learn where they came from. This will help to heal from the trigger itself, but also with healing from our trauma. Knowledge is power, and by understanding where a trigger comes from and why it is bubbling to the surface, we can analyze it and start working through it. This played a massive role in my healing journey. I'm not asking you to do anything I haven't done, but I warn you this can be emotionally painful to walk through. One example was when memories from being my daughter's age started coming up and were still affecting me. (We'll continue to talk about this trigger throughout both the mindset tool and the EQ tool). That's a long time to be triggered by something that you didn't realize was still an issue. I used a technique from my friend Noble Gibbens.[11]

The first thing that I want you to do is to make a list of what triggers you. What situations or statements create an immediate and overwhelming mountain of emotions? Write them down. And then I want you to take them one at a time. The task for this exercise is to try to figure out what the origin story is for each trigger. When was the very first time you felt this way? In this example, the story that I remembered started as a teenager, but at that point, my reaction was already to shut down. So I had to keep going further back to the very first time. What made me shut down as a teen and become so triggered as an adult? When I went back through memory lane, not only did I understand where it came from, but I could see all the emotions tied to this one trigger and how I responded to it. I was able to see that my fear and misunderstanding created thoughts that became lies. Eventually, I would repeat the fear and lies that would trigger me every time a similar event happened.

So, we are going to find the origin story (the first time you experienced this) and try to remember how it made you feel. It's hard to look at how a younger version of you received and believed something, but it will help! Work to understand your emotions and what you have been telling yourself whenever it comes up again. As we talked about in the last chapter, when we identify our negative thoughts and change them to positive ones, our brain believes them more. We can take the lie we've told ourselves and reverse it to be a positive truth about ourselves. It is very difficult to change our thoughts about ourselves, and I often still get challenged by my closest people when I start repeating a lie about myself that I've believed all these years. But the good news is that even when I say the lie and they challenge me, I'm at least no longer fighting with them about why I believed that lie was true. I'm to the point that I can say, "I know, but sometimes it's still challenging to change how you've always seen yourself or how people in your life made you feel your whole life." And it certainly is! But I'm doing it, and you can too!!!

EQ Tool

While we're working through our triggers and the emotions each trigger brings, it's helpful to analyze the event and emotions. We want to decide if the emotions are bringing any value to our lives. I've already said how much I enjoy listening to my friend Noble Gibbens' podcast, *EQ Gangster.*[12] He posts weekly, and I carry many learning morsels from his show! One of them is the tool for this chapter. During this specific podcast, he was working through a mission trip he and his family had just taken. He worked through several questions. He recommends journaling the questions and working through them several times to achieve the best result for each question. Here are some of the questions he asked:

- What is this feeling telling me?
- How can I learn from it?
- How can I do better? (without judgment but from a view of learning)
- What is God trying to show me through this emotion?

So, to use his format, let me tell you about one of my triggers. If I can get very real in this already very vulnerable book, one of the biggest triggers I had to work through was being talked over or interrupted. For most people, this does not seem like a huge earth-shattering thing; for me, it was. All my life, people have interrupted, talked over, and really not even listened to me. It goes all the way back to the early years of elementary school when I remember feeling as if what I had to say was not important enough for anyone to listen to. As I became a teen and more hot-tempered, I would attempt no more than twice to say what I wanted, and if I kept getting interrupted, I would just stop. You wouldn't hear another word of significance from me for the rest of the day or night. Even if asked, I would just say that it was not important or lie and say that I had forgotten what I was planning to say, which was very seldom the truth. It happened more times than I think it really should; it felt like a commonplace occurrence. The lies that I told myself grew deeper and sank down into my core beliefs about myself. And yes, I do still struggle with believing why anyone would want to listen to anything I have to say. So, let's use this triggering event to work through these questions.

The trigger: *being interrupted and getting very angry about it.*

- What is this feeling telling me?

Being angry means that one or more of my rights have been infringed upon or my needs are not being met. Most people agree that one of the basic human rights is equality. Let me define equality. We are all created by God. As God's creation, we are all equal. I believe we should treat everyone with respect and value because we are all sons and daughters of the Lord Most High! For me, I did not feel respect or value. It was very hurtful because I didn't know why people did this, and most of the time, I thought the person loved me. So, when someone you think loves you or is "supposed" to love you constantly treats you disrespectfully, you start to feel that they know something you don't know and are right to treat you this way. Even typing it out, I feel so sad for the younger me who felt this way. I look at my own children and pray that I can help them never to feel this way. So, the feeling tells me I'm not being respected.

- How can I learn from it?

I can probably learn that this is not about me. It is about the other person and their need or desire to be heard or seen. They probably don't see what it has done or is doing to me. I can learn that I should tell people how their actions or words make me feel. I can learn to be more assertive and stand up for myself instead of just shutting down. I also think that Satan thrives on situations like this because he enjoys the lies that we tell ourselves; he loves to separate people, and he takes pleasure in shutting down discussions that could bond, teach, or help encourage the participants of the conversation.

- How can I do better?

I think the best way to do better is to learn how to control my anger so that I can teach my children differently. I want to ensure I don't unintentionally or unknowingly do the same thing to them. I think that I can do better by getting myself under control. This will help me not continue this pattern, be more aware, and give each person respect and value.

- What is God trying to show me through this emotion?

God is trying to show me how it feels to be disrespected and insignificant. I think it's essential with my work to help me empathize with where people are. If I cannot show respect or be courteous to others, I will not be able to show up for them in the way they need. I also think healing from this trigger has helped me be more loving and compassionate as a mom, aunt, daughter, friend, and leader. If we allow God to use the bad things that happen to us, He can and will use all things in all ways.

This does not have to be what your answers look like. And honestly, I was not at all in this space when I was first working through this trigger. At the time of writing this, I think I am about 18 months past the first time I worked on this specific trigger for myself.

I do not discount how difficult these two tools are to work through. I often said it felt like my brain had just gotten done in a boxing match. I felt so emotionally drained and tired after working on my triggers. I'm still not perfect, but I am way better than before.

Biblical Promise

"Trust in the Lord with all your heart and lean not on your own understanding; in all your ways submit to Him, and He will make your paths straight."
Proverbs 3:5-6

I think that one of the toughest challenges we face as Christians is being able to live by the Spirit and not by the flesh. We are trying to live how God wants and has instructed us to. Many of Paul's teachings are about being able to live by the Spirit and not the flesh. This Proverb helps us to understand why. When we are able to submit ourselves to God's leading, we will be greatly successful in how we live our lives. Our society tells us how much we deserve things and how much we need to live our own lives. However, the Bible teaches the opposite. Really, when we think of everything that God has done for us and Jesus dying on the cross for us, we should be thanking God for not giving us what we deserve! We are all sinners, even when we are trying our best to follow the Spirit's leading and instruction. When we lean on God, His ways, and His Spirit, we become more compassionate, respectful, and loving than when we are trying to do it all on our own.

The big question remains, though: "How do we trust in the Lord with all our heart?" This is tricky because I know what it looks like or feels like for me, but I've heard many stories of God talking to others in ways that I have never experienced. So, what it looks like for you may be different, and that's ok! Not everyone has to be the same. But I do believe that God reveals His plan, or at least a portion of His plan, for us to follow. He could show you by a constant thought of something that you normally would not think about, you could hear an audible direction, or you could have a dream several nights in a row that you can't get out of your head. God can talk to us in so many different ways. We first have to know that it is from God. A few good ways to do this are to pray about it, ask others to pray with you, and read the scriptures to see if they agree with what you feel your task is. Once you've confirmed that it is truly from God, the next step is to obey His instructions. And that can be terribly scary! But when I get scared about it, I pray. I just keep praying. I ask that God give me peace. I ask that God protect me from Satan's whispering lies; I pray that, since this is His will for me, He takes it and blesses it. There are so many things that I pray for, trying to be in obedience to Him and His plan for my life. It's so difficult sometimes, and I struggle with not feeling good enough, but I want to be a good and faithful servant of the Lord!

The best way to avoid setting ourselves up for failure is to "Trust in the Lord with all your heart and lean not on your own understanding; in all your ways submit to Him, and He will make your paths straight." It's not easy, but leaning on God through prayer, the prayers of others, and searching scripture will give you peace and strength when you submit to Him!

Grief through Grace

Thoughts, Prayers, or Takeaways

_____

_____

_____

_____

_____

_____

_____

_____

_____

_____

_____

_____

_____

_____

_____

_____

_____

_____

_____

_____

_____

_____

_____

_____

Chapter 6
Trusting God Through It All

"You will keep in perfect peace those whose minds are steadfast because they trust in You. Trust in the Lord forever, for the Lord, the Lord himself, is the Rock eternal." Isaiah 26:3-4

I think it was about a year after Keith passed away that I was so completely broken in my grief that I called out to God and asked Him why I was on this path. Why do I have to endure this? Why do my children have to grow up without their father? Why does it have to be me? Clear as day, I heard God say back to me, without missing a beat, "I need you on this path over here, and you wouldn't have been able to be on this path with Keith here." Now, I don't think that God killed my husband. Keith knew that he had a heart condition, and he made the choice of a poor diet and not following up with a cardiologist. He knew that he should, but he was too afraid. However, I also know that God could have healed Keith while they worked on him, and he would have come through the procedure. I also know that God could have changed Keith's heart so I could be on the path God has put me on. However, I'm not sure I would have moved out of my comfort zone to be here. It has been a long process for me to take ownership of saying that with Keith, I would not have checked in with my mindset or where God was pushing me to go. I probably would have felt the Holy Spirit tugging on my heart, but I probably would have opted not to have an uncomfortable conversation, assuming I'd know what Keith would say. Most of the time, when I tell people that I've heard God speak to me and directly answer my question, I get looks of amazement at how incredible it is. People long for God to answer them or speak clearly to them personally. And I agree, it's incredible, but I've also found it absolutely terrifying at times. What in the world am I supposed to do that is so important that my husband had to die for it? There's been a lot of fighting with God about my plan and purpose, and sometimes, I think I don't want to go down this pathway and put myself out here like this. I am really a private person, and sharing my heart, as I have done in this book, is really uncomfortable. I have too much on my plate just to raise these two children by myself.

In 2017, I started working through a Biblical and Educational Studies program. I loved learning more about God and how He wants me to live and raise Charlotte. I had a good schedule of praying and meditating. I was in the Word daily and felt like I was getting to where I was supposed to be as a Christian. One night, I was struggling in prayer with an idea I had for several years for my church. The only problem was that it was a vast project, and no one knew how to start it. I felt like it had been put on my heart for many years, and I was wrestling with not wanting to head this project because I had no qualifications. I also felt like several others in our church were much better suited and skilled at making this idea work.

It was dark; I was praying before I fell asleep, and I had a vision of a person standing before a blinding light. He told me I needed to be strong; He was with me, but the hardest was not over yet. I assumed that He was talking about this project with the church. Looking back, I think Jesus was trying to prepare me for what would happen in the next year. I'm honestly not sure if I would have been able to lean so closely on God if I didn't have that experience. I truly believe that Jesus came to me in this vision to prepare me for what was coming and to strengthen my faith. I also think praying daily with focused and intentional time with the Lord greatly grew my faith.

After Keith passed away, I couldn't stay focused enough to pray or meditate. I once told my pastor how much I was struggling with even being able to say simple prayers. He told me that he finds comfort in the fact that when he can't pray, he knows others are praying for him. That thought was a comfort for me. This is a hugely important thought; even in the depths of our pain and grief, several people will rally around you to pray when you need it and when you can't pray for yourself. If you don't feel like you have people in your life who can or will pray for you, there is a section on my website where you can add your prayer requests, and I have a team of people who will pray for you![13]

There have been so many times in the past six years when I have been able to see God working in my life. I won't go over all of them here, but I will say that it is really cool when I start to follow God's direction and can see Him working in real-time. All too often, we see God's hand in hindsight. When we look for what He is doing in our lives right now, we begin to trust God more.

In late 2019 or early 2020, I started to feel like I was supposed to write this book. I fought with God so much because I didn't want to write a book. This is not how I identified, allowing myself to be put out there like that. After several months of trying to ignore this pull, I finally told my mom that I felt God had put this book on my heart, but I didn't want to write it. I told her, "This is not who I am; no one will want to read or hear anything I say." My mom thought it was a great idea and started encouraging me to write. Since I started writing this book (even though it has taken way longer than I think it should have), God has been showing me clear and concise paths for me to walk down: starting my journey to get my coaching credentials, meeting my business partner, and all the many people who have helped me along the way with my path and plan. They all arrived in my life after I started writing this book. I often felt like, apart from being a mom and an active church member, my life had no other meaning or purpose. I no longer feel that way. Once I started coaching, and especially when I began teaching others how to coach, I finally felt like this was what I was created to do. My purpose is to lead others to Christ and help others through the tragedies that I have endured. And I'm no longer struggling with this call anymore. I trust God no matter what is thrown at me; He will get me through!

Mindset Change

So often, we get stuck in the pain of what happened to us that we can't see past it to view it from a different perspective. However, if we can change our perspective on why something happened to us, it can create a sense of peace within us. This peace will lead to healing. We can ask ourselves some questions to help find a different way to look at the events.

- How can I use this? Can you see any kind of purpose in what has happened?

I agree that there is no purpose in my husband's dying, but I can decide to use the pain for something good. By shifting this thought, I am able to find my purpose. The pain or the tragedy itself doesn't hold the purpose, but because I am willing to use it, that action gives me purpose.

- What positive meaning do you want this event to have?

We get to decide the meaning something places on our lives. Some of the answers you might give are:

- "It means I'm resilient and strong."
- "It means that I will do better for others."
- "It means I'll stand up and protect it from happening to others."

By shifting our thinking from the "what ifs" and "what could have been" to "how can I make good from this?" we are better able to focus on trusting Jesus, which leads to peace.

EQ Tool

I really like breathing exercises, and I think they are an excellent way to help our minds and bodies calm down when we're overstimulated, stressed, angry, or anything else. Regardless of what they are, big emotions cloud our minds, preventing us from seeing things in a clear light. We often do things while we're clouded that we regret later. But we often don't have the time for a long, drawn-out exercise for whatever reason. So, I like to teach this breathing exercise for those times when there's simply not much time to regain control of our emotions. It is called Hot Cocoa Breathing, and I learned it from a Treating Trauma and PTSD course by Alan Fayter.

If you're able, close your eyes. Imagine holding a delicious cup of hot cocoa, steam billowing out of the mug in your hands. It's still too hot to drink, so you'll breathe in the smell long and slow and then blow on the liquid to cool it down. This is not a hard and fast breath out because if you have a steaming cup of cocoa, you'd splash it everywhere if you blew hard and fast on it. It's a slow and steady breath out, just like you're trying to cool your delicious drink to be able to enjoy it. Repeat this breath in and out as many times as you have time for or until you're feeling calm. Perhaps it sounds silly and too simple, but it really helps if you're in the right mindset to allow it, so I invite you to try it for yourself before you decide.

Biblical Promise

"You will keep in perfect peace those whose minds are steadfast, because they trust in You. Trust in the Lord forever, for the Lord, the Lord himself, is the Rock eternal." Isaiah 26:3-4

Isaiah was a prophet who primarily appealed to Israel, with a special focus on the tribe of Judah. The beginning of the book is a reprimand for turning away from God. The second part of the book is filled with hope and love! It's a very difficult thing for us to put our faith and trust in the Lord. It was then, and it still is now.

Even though it's a rather tricky thing to do, there are still many stories in the Bible that highlight people trusting in God's plan, even when their lives were on the line. Noah is a great example. God told him to build an ark, provided the measurements, and said that animals would come and the world would be flooded. His friends and neighbors laughed at him. Noah still trusted God, and God saved humanity through him.

Esther put her actual life on the line when her husband passed a law that the Jewish people could be killed. Her cousin said, "Who knows if perhaps you were made queen for such a time as this." Esther 4:14. She was so afraid that she asked her cousin, all his relatives, and all her attendants in the castle to fast with her for three days. Esther asked God to reprieve her and then trusted that He would.

Job had everything taken from him except his wife. His land, his animals, all his children, and even his health were gone. His lovely friends told him just to curse God and die. He never turned his back on God! He did not say anything against Him.

In the New Testament, Paul takes trusting God to a whole new level. He immediately turned from being one of the most feared persecutors of Christians to being one of the best advocates for the Christian religion. Paul was often thrown into jail, and he was stoned. There were many times when he had to flee for his life. Even when he was in prison, he was a witness to those around him. The guards with whom he shared Jesus while imprisoned went on to start their own churches.

All these stories show great faith, and I know that with most of them, I'd be scared out of my mind if I had to walk in any of their shoes. We can learn and follow their examples because of their bravery, trust, and obedience in the Lord. When we learn to have steadfast minds and trust in the Lord, no matter what turmoil we are facing, we will also have perfect peace!

Grief through Grace

Thoughts, Prayers, or Takeaways

Chapter 7

Self-Doubt

"Do not be anxious about anything, but in every situation, by prayer and petition, with thanksgiving, present your requests to the Lord. And the peace of God, which transcends all understanding, will guard your hearts and your minds in Christ Jesus."
Philippians 4:6-7.

Harvard Business Review loosely defines *impostor syndrome* as "doubting your abilities and feeling like a fraud."[14] Impostor syndrome is something that I have struggled with my whole life. I have countless learning ailments that hinder me from being a top student. Learning has always been challenging. Whenever there was something that I excelled at, I thought it was a fluke or that someone better just hadn't shown up yet. Even outside the academic world, as an adolescent and young adult, I consistently excelled. Starting with my very first job in high school, before I even graduated, I was training, scheduling, and ordering everything for the substation inside the little store where I worked. When I left and went to work for other companies and organizations, I consistently performed well. I always learned as much as possible, did my best, and taught others when the time came.

But still, even with all of that, the voice in my head takes me back to first grade when my teacher made a point to show the whole class that my coloring page was the worst in the class and that I was nowhere near the best in the class. I turn into that little girl who was repeatedly told that she would not amount to anything and would never learn to read. Through the years and the times when I was cut down by people in my life, I began to understand that I was not someone who would do well in life or achieve great things. People would listen to me talk about things that I'm passionate about and tell me that I should become a speaker. I would laugh and say that no one wants to hear me speak about anything. When I started coaching, I fought everyone's praise of my abilities, patience, and steadiness. It has taken me a long time and work to be more confident in myself. Even now, I still very often argue with my business partner and my current coach about how I am not qualified for something. I'm not sure if the impostor syndrome will ever go away. And it doesn't matter much what you call it; self-doubt is one of the biggest weapons that Satan uses against us.

Several years ago, I decided that I didn't want to take part in the idea of New Year's Resolutions. Instead, I entered the new year focusing on a word or a phrase. This allowed me to assess where I was and where I wanted to be as a person, mom, friend, daughter, and so on. For around two to three years after Keith passed, my word was *grace*. I wanted to learn how to have grace for myself, for others, and for the circumstances surrounding me. I believe it has made me a more patient and understanding person. In 2021, I don't remember what my word was, but the year ended up being a year of "do it afraid." So many things happened in 2021 that I was so afraid to go through, but I didn't want to live my life based on fear.

In February, I decided to see if I was a candidate for Lasik eye surgery. In the beginning, I was not at all afraid. Since I was about 20, I said that if I were to get cosmetic surgery, I think Lasik would be the only one, or at least the first one, I'd really be interested in. As time went on with scheduling appointments and waiting, fear began to creep in. I spoke with a friend who had it done; when I asked him about his experience, his response was straightforward. "Lasik? Do it." I said, "Well, I don't know if I can yet. I still have to go and make sure that I'm eligible." He responded with, "You will be; do it." After that, I felt a little better about my decision, but I was still nervous.

When I met with the doctor to verify that I could have Lasik, I asked what the chances were that I would go blind from this. He said that I won't. I just looked at him without really believing him. I had experienced having a husband die on an operating table with a 5% chance that anything would go wrong. He saw my distrust and tried explaining why I wouldn't go blind. I honestly don't remember what he said, but he did try to explain it to me.

The day of the surgery, I was sitting there, waiting for my turn. I was still so scared, and I kept looking at my girls' pictures. I was so afraid that I'd never see them again, but I kept thinking that it would be so much better for me if I no longer had to wear glasses. Many people told me it was wonderful and that I should do it. I did go through with it. I prayed and prayed, asking God to please allow me to leave after the procedure with my sight. He was merciful, and I still have my eyesight today. Still, to this day, I feel like making that choice and getting the surgery was the best thing that I have ever done just for myself.

In April, I had the opportunity of a lifetime. My mom

had signed up for a continuing education course and, with it, was given a coach. Towards the end, he asked her if she knew anything about coaching before this. She told him that she had only heard of it because I had changed my major and wanted to become a coach after completing my degree. But she did not know what it meant. Not long after that, we both received emails about a fantastic opportunity to join a class that would teach us how to become international coaches. The invitation email arrived on Thursday, and classes were scheduled to start the following Monday. The plan was to meet three times a week for one-hour sessions. I had a four-year-old and a two-year-old at home. I immediately went into panic mode and had just stopped my schoolwork because I started homeschooling after COVID hit. After all, all the schools were closed. I had no clue how I could dedicate so much time to a program when these two little ones still needed me so much. This opportunity would give me exactly what I wanted to do as a career much faster than I thought I could initially do it; I still really struggled with deciding if it was feasible for me and my family. There was also a lot of impostor syndrome associated with it: "Will people see me as qualified to do this work if I don't have a degree saying that I can do it?" When we're almost programmed to see and believe the worst about ourselves, it's really hard to turn that narrative off and see all of the possibilities.

Gratefully, I went through the program with Two Roads Leadership (now called Flatter Leadership Academy) by Flatter, Inc. They have a great coaching program and have trained so many incredible coaches through all their programs. I am absolutely blessed to be able to count myself among those who they have trained. It was hard, I won't say that it wasn't. I relied on my family and friends for support during the first few months of my training. I feel that I have done an excellent job of learning the best I could, and I will continue to learn. I have pushed through and accomplished my goals to be internationally credentialed, and from the outside, I look like I'm very successful with all of it. Internally, however, I still often worry whether I'm good enough or if I am serving each of my clients in the best way. I no longer feel like I must have the degree to qualify myself. I often think about returning to school to get a degree, but it would no longer be work-related but instead related to my faith.

So often, for me, my self-doubt manifests as fear. Even as I write this chapter and nearly finish the book, I find myself stalled and procrastinating. I have been fed lines of fear from the enemy on every level in the last month; everything, from I'm not a good mom, friend, daughter, Christian, etc., so if I publish this book, it will bomb, and I will be judged by it. If I publish this book, everyone will know all the garbage that I carry around, and I'm exposing myself too much. There are so many fears that I have never even had that have come up in the time of writing out these last few chapters. At some point, we must decide to pick ourselves up by our bootstraps and say that I'm going to do it, despite the fear. I've had to remind myself of why I initially decided to write this book. If even one person can get something out of it, or my experience can help in someone else's healing journey, that's enough for me. This is a constant reminder that I tell myself as I'm swimming over here in all this fear. If this book can aid just one person, that is absolutely enough; it will all be worth it! If you have something that you are so afraid to do, make that jump, and do it afraid! Don't allow your self-doubt to hold you back! We are our own worst critics, and Satan plays on what we already tell ourselves.

Mindset Change

As I have many times before, I'm going to ask some questions to help you change your current, fearful thinking (or at least, for me, it's fearful thinking!) And yes, this is what I did to work through all my fears. It's challenging to push through negative thoughts, but if we can take some deep breaths, such as box breathing, and maintain an open mind, we can start to feel better. Afterwards, asking these questions will help! I will answer them for myself in this situation as an example.

- What would your life look like if your self-doubt didn't hold you back?

Well, I probably would have created a much different life for myself in my late teens or early twenties. Currently, it would look like a thriving company where I could help people with their grief and speak to people about God, leadership, compassion, resiliency, and teamwork. I would be a successful published author and maybe even have more than one book written. I'd be living a life on fire for our Lord and Savior!

- What positive narrative can you say to help yourself?

I have been telling myself that God put this book on my heart and won't let me forget about it. I remind myself that friends and family have read parts of the book, and when others hear the book's concept, they all say that this book is so needed and will be helpful to so many people (God willing, this is my prayer). I pray and ask Jesus to shield me from Satan, whispering in my ears and telling me lies, and to help me push through all my fears! I continue to pray that He helps me do His will. I say that I want to be used by Him and to please help me get out of my own way so that my life can be what He wants it to be. I return to the Bible's promises to help me overcome my negative thinking and self-doubt.

- What would celebrating yourself look like?

For me, it often looks like just telling my mom or one of my close friends about the accomplishment. So, when I finally finish this chapter after being stalled for over a month in fear, I'll be sending messages to my close people to tell them that I'm finally done!! And I'll feel a virtual pat on the back as they celebrate with me!

If you are not in the right frame of mind, these questions may seem pointless or ineffective. If you find yourself in that space, you might revisit some of the other mindset change sections, or you can set it aside for a while and come back when you're ready. When I was pretty low, I rolled my eyes at them, and I'm the one who wrote them as the tool!! Trust me, I absolutely get it! But I also wanted to try to get myself in a more emotionally regulated state, and then I came back. It took a few days. But I reached out to my people and was honest with them about how I was feeling, even though it was ugly. And even though they pushed back to say that my thinking wasn't correct, by pushing back against them, I was able to understand why I was feeling so low and how I needed to regulate myself. Discussing my thoughts and feelings with close friends helped me prepare and then answer these questions. I will never tell you that any of this is emotionally easy, but it will help you work through it in the long run.

EQ Tool

So far, I've discussed all intellectual tools and how to put yourself into a different mood or thought process. One of the things many people don't like to hear, though, is how valuable it is to move our bodies when we are feeling stressed, overwhelmed, uncertain, or confused. Being able to have a physical release of those emotions is very beneficial! And we are often able to look at things differently while our bodies have more oxygen due to the movement. I usually just go for a walk when I'm feeling stuck or uncertain about a thought. Just by changing the scenery when we are feeling stuck, or when we are angry about whatever, or confused about where to go now, we can see what's going on from a different light.

Another thing to consider with physical activity is how it helps us to release our emotions and trauma. In the book, "The Body Keeps the Score,"[15] Bessel A. van der Kolk talks about the physical effect that trauma puts on our body, how we go into fight, flight, or freeze mode during a situation that our brain perceives as a threat, and often how we are unable to release the body's hold on it, which prevents us from healing completely. There is much scientific evidence that van der Kolk uses for the book to show the connection between the brain and the body. He recommends yoga to help release the emotions from the body. I'm not a huge fan of yoga, so whether you want to do yoga, take a walk, or do a HIIT (high-intensity interval training) workout, to name a few, it will all help your body move through the emotions of what has happened to you and allow you to come out of the fight, flight, or freeze state. I also understand that many people have physical limitations, and I want to address that as well.

While in the editing process of this book, I was diagnosed with an auto-immune disease, and it has completely taken a toll on my body and my mobility. So, I can sympathize with limited mobility also. On the days that I'm struggling and feeling stuck but also don't physically feel like I can walk, I will often go outside and stand barefoot in the grass and sun for like 3-5 minutes to allow the sun, the sounds of birds, and nature, and the feel of the grass on my feet to fill my senses and try to release all of the negative energy that I'm holding. Other options for bad pain days would be chair or bed stretching or exercises. You can find many low-impact exercise videos on YouTube or other social media outlets. And let's not forget about how valuable the breathing exercises are. They are exercises, too, and they help with breathing rate, heart rate, and mental clarity.

Biblical Promise

"Do not be anxious about anything, but in every situation, by prayer and petition, with thanksgiving, present your request to the Lord. And the peace of God, which transcends all understanding, will guard your heart and your mind in Christ Jesus."
Philippians 4:6-7

"Do not be afraid" or "Fear not" is said over 100 times in the Bible. There is controversy about how many actual times, but still, the Bible tells us numerous times not to fear. I do, however, know that it is easier said than done. John 10:10 says, "The thief comes only to steal and kill and destroy." Satan is actively working to capitalize on our fears and turn them into anxiety so that the fears can fester and grow inside of us. The devil delights in our mistrust of God, and he is working against us every step of the way to create distance and a wedge in our relationship with the Lord. So, the big question is, if evil forces are working so hard against us, and if it is so difficult to "not be anxious about anything," how do we put that into practice in our everyday lives? The next couple of verses in Philippians tell us precisely what to do to truly "Fear not."

Grief through Grace

Verses 8-9 says, "Finally, brothers and sisters, whatever is **true**, whatever is **noble**, whatever is **right**, whatever is **pure**, whatever is **lovely**, whatever is **admirable** – if anything is **excellent** or **praiseworthy** – think about such things. Whatever you have learned or received or heard from me or seen in me – put it into practice. And the God of peace will be with you."

A common talking point for many people for the past several years is having a gratitude journal. The idea is that if we start or end our day with the things for which we are grateful, we are less likely to focus on the bad things in life. This is one part, but exactly what Philippians 4:8-9 is telling us is to look at our lives and, instead of only seeing all the terrible things going on, see the beauty and the good that is happening too. "Think on such things." When we focus on these things and put them into practice in our lives, "the God of peace will be with you."

I know it can be daunting to find things to be grateful for when you're in the thick of grief. The first thing that I could feel thankful for was that I didn't have to sleep with the television on anymore. It wasn't the kids or all the happy things I experienced with my first pregnancy. All those things caused me more pain that I couldn't see past. It was something small and minor, insignificant even. Often, these are the things we can start with when we are in the trenches of grief. Below is a list of things I am grateful for. I thought it might help you create your list.

- The beauty of a flower
- The warmth of the sun
- The laughter of a child
- Birds
- Friends and family
- Church Family

- The silliness of a dog
- The purring of a cat
- Food to eat
- Pillow and blanket
- Fresh air to breathe
- Water to drink
- Music

There are, of course, so many more things that we can be grateful for. That's just a small list. But it is a good starting point if you're struggling to find other things to be grateful for. Or, you could be like me, who took way too long to realize that I no longer have to sleep with the TV on and allow that to start your journey to peace.

Grief through Grace

Thoughts, Prayers, or Takeaways

_____
_____
_____
_____
_____
_____
_____
_____
_____
_____
_____
_____
_____
_____
_____
_____
_____
_____
_____
_____
_____
_____

Chapter 8

The 3 R's

A colleague, Winsome Culley of "The Positive Vibes Radio Show,"[16] does an exercise every new year. He works through questions of reflection, refocusing, and releasing. I think this is an incredible way to check in with what's going on and how you're doing. What needs to be changed, and what should remain the same? With Winsome's permission and the help of my personal coach, Christine Rabaja, I have changed his questions to be more related to grief and healing. I will answer the questions for myself so you can see how it goes, and then I'll give space for you to work through these questions. Even if you're unable to answer the questions at this point, let them sit for a few days or weeks and come back to them.

Reflect

- What energizes you (activities, people, etc.)? What drains you?

I think the biggest thing that energizes me is being one-on-one with friends. I get overwhelmed and overstimulated easily, so it's often very taxing on me to be in a big crowd, even with my own people. But spending quality time with one person at a time is always very uplifting to me. Some of the other things that really give me a pick-me-up in the day are talking about topics that I'm passionate about, studying scripture, and learning!

Equally, being around too many people drains me, and being asked too many questions is even worse. I often find myself in this situation, and while I don't necessarily mind it, it is very draining. Once I get home from whatever it is, I like to sit in a dark, quiet room for a little bit to regulate back out.

- Think about your life; what has had real meaning?

Being a mom is probably the job that gives me the most meaning. I loved being a wife, too. I love all my jobs at church, too. And I think teaching is another thing I have found an incredible amount of meaning and purpose in.

- If nothing changes, what are you sacrificing?

If nothing changes from where I'm at right now, I'll sacrifice all the dreams I built by myself. After learning how to let go of the dreams of life that Keith and I had, it took me a while to figure out what I wanted my life to look like. If nothing from this moment changes, all that goes away.

<u>Refocus</u>

- How will you take care of yourself better this year? List several things.

My top priority will be regaining control over my health. I've allowed a few things to go while working on this book, and I will go back to being "strong, fit, and healthy." I will visit a couple of doctors to address various ailments that I have been struggling with. I am also starting the practice of

The 3 R's

"What's your favorite thing that happened today?" at dinner time. And that allows the brain to look for something good that has happened, which I think will have a good impact on the girls, too.

- Think about what you're passionate about. What do you feel so strongly about that you're willing to take a risk for?

This book is probably the most significant thing for a while, and I've been so passionate about it that I'm willing to risk a lot for it. This has been a difficult book for me to write emotionally, and at every turn, it has brought up a range of emotions that I genuinely thought I had already worked through and healed from. I have taken other risks during this grief process, but completing this book and pushing forward to get it published is definitely the most considerable risk I'm taking.

- What would it look like if you started a feelings journal?

Knowing your feelings and understanding where they are coming from has many benefits. I currently do not track them. However, I do think there is a benefit. I could see trends in my emotions or when I'm struggling with something to try to pick up on it faster. When I have an understanding of what I am feeling, I can get things back under control and resolve them.

Release

- What would you like to let go of? What would it take to make that happen?

Probably the hardest thing for me to let go of is the feeling that I'm failing as a mom. I am better at not thinking that I'm a terrible mom, but I still often feel like I'm losing it and, therefore, failing them.

I think I need to revisit affirmations to make that happen. I have used affirmations successfully in the past, and I think that starting them up again will help.

- How will you give yourself permission to grieve while still accomplishing your goals?

Well, I definitely don't recommend the "just push through it" method. That has gotten me into trouble more than I'd like to admit... I think the best way for me is to examine the emotions and try to understand where they are coming from. And then talking about it with either my mom, coach, or business partner has really helped me to still be able to grieve while writing this but keep moving forward.

- How do you define and acknowledge healing milestones?

Fuller Life Family Therapy defines healing milestones as things that "allow individuals to adapt to changed circumstances, accept reality, restore well-being, and integrate grief into one's life experiences." However, I do feel like finishing this book is another healing milestone for me. I believe that the act of writing has brought deeper healing. And this definition does not have to be yours; you can define healing milestones in any way you want. But I had to look it up because I really didn't know.

And now it's your turn.

The 3 R's

<u>Reflect</u>

- What energizes you (activities, people, etc.)?

_____
_____
_____
_____
_____
_____

- What drains you?

_____
_____
_____
_____
_____
_____

- Think about your life; what has had real meaning?

_____
_____
_____
_____
_____
_____

- If nothing changes, what are you sacrificing?

_____
_____
_____
_____
_____
_____

Grief through Grace

Refocus

- How will you take care of yourself better this year? List several things.

_____

- Think about what you're passionate about. What do you feel so strongly about that you're willing to take a risk for?

_____

- What would it look like if you started a feelings journal?

_____

84

The 3 R's

<u>Release</u>

- What would you like to let go of?

_____

_____

_____

_____

_____

_____

- What would it take to make that happen?

_____

_____

_____

_____

_____

- How will you give yourself permission to grieve while still accomplishing your goals?

_____

_____

_____

_____

_____

- How do you define and acknowledge healing milestones?

_____

_____

_____

_____

_____

Acknowledgments

Above all, I give my thanks to Jesus Christ, my Lord and Savior, for His guidance and blessings throughout this journey.

I am profoundly grateful to:

Diane Moncrief
Christine Rabaja
Cam Macias
Angela Baxter
Michelle Turdici
Rachael Petschke
Sue Comfort
Erin Scheibe

Thank you for your invaluable prayers, constant encouragement, and tireless dedication in helping me refine this work. Your belief in me has meant the world, and I am forever in your debt.

References

1 Good Questions Have Groups Talking - Luke Bible Study. (n.d.). https://www.mybiblestudylessons.com/Luke2012

2 Welcome to ICF: International Coaching Federation. ICF. (2025, May 19). https://coachingfederation.org/

3 Dweck, Carol S. *Mindset: The New Psychology of Success.* Ballantine Books, 2016.

4 Willcox, G. (1982). The Feeling Wheel: A Tool for Expanding Awareness of Emotions and Increasing Spontaneity and Intimacy. Transactional Analysis Journal, 12(4), 274–276. https://doi.org/10.1177/036215378201200411

5 J. Fellowes, "A Journey to the Highlands," Downton Abbey, season 3, episode directed by Andy Goddard, aired December 25, 2012.

6 G. Gibbs, *Learning by Doing: A Guide to Teaching and Learning Methods*, Further Education Unit at Oxford Polytechnic, UK, 1998.

7 N. McInerny, We don't "Move on" from grief. we move forward with it. TED. https://www.ted.com/talks/nora_mcinerny_we_don_t_move_on_from_grief_we_move_forward_with_it

8 Noble Gibbens, *EQ Gangster*, Apple Podcasts, podcasts.apple.com/us/podcast/eq-gangster/id1497445408. Accessed 27 May 2025.

9   Joyce Meyer, *Battlefield of the Mind: Winning The Battle in Your Mind*. Faith Words, Hachette Book Group, 2025.

10   They'll Know We Are Christians by our Love," Peter Scholtes, © 1966, F.E.L. Publications, assigned to The Lorenz Corp., 1991, https://hymnary.org/text/we_are_one_in_the_spirit

11   *EQ Gangster*

12   ibid

13   Pressedcoal.org

14   Tulshyan, R., & Burey, J.-A. (2021, February 11). Stop telling women they have impostor syndrome. Harvard Business Review. https://hbr.org/2021/02/stop-telling-women-they-have-impostor-syndrome

15   van der Kolk, B., & Pratt, S. (2021). The body keeps the score bessel van der kolk. Penguin Random House Audio Publishing Group.

16   Positivevibes Radio. PositiveVibes Radio. (n.d.). https://www.positivevibesradioshow.com/

About the Author

Stephanie Lodor is a devoted Christian, passionate coach, and loving mother from the Midwest. With a heart for service, she volunteers at her local church. As a dedicated homeschool mom, she also teaches at a homeschool co-op, nurturing young minds with faith and wisdom.

Certified as a Professional Certified Coach (PCC) by the International Coaching Federation (ICF), Stephanie excels in fostering deep connections and facilitating transformative workshops. Her expertise extends to being an Everything DiSC Certified Practitioner and a Coaching Culture Facilitator.

When she's not empowering others through her coaching, Stephanie finds joy in the great outdoors, embracing activities like hiking and canoeing. Her book reflects her profound belief in the power of faith, family, and personal growth.

Find her online at pressedcoal.org.

www.ingramcontent.com/pod-product-compliance
Lightning Source LLC
Chambersburg PA
CBHW051227120626
46547CB00013B/1542